Touchstone

****

Touchstone

****

BEATRICE W. SIMS

Best wishes to Charles & Marjorie —
Eagles Mere, 1997

Bea Sims

SUTTER HOUSE

1997

LIBRARY OF CONGRESS CATALOGING-IN-PUBLICATION DATA
Sims, Beatrice W., 1921–
        Touchstone / Beatrice W. Sims
            p.   cm.
        ISBN 0-915010-40-2 (pbk.)
        I. Title.
    PS3569.I5177T68   1996
    811' .54--dc   2196-44494
                                            CIP

MANUFACTURED IN THE UNITED STATES OF AMERICA

Designed and published by
Sutter House
P.O. Box 212
Lititz, Pa. 17543

❋

The written word

should be clean as a bone

clear as light

firm as stone.

Two words are not

as good as one.

ANONYMOUS

CONTENTS

ONE

"AND THEN THERE WAS MORNING"

The Hidden

The Dry Wall

Wind Blown

The Storm

Gifts

The Cache

Kaleidoscope

Patterns

Alina Lodge

November

New Day Sonnet

The Tree

✺ THE HIDDEN ✺

My indoor carpets
are not fine.
My outdoor carpets
needled pine.
Walk with me . . .

Stones covering
the mountain spring
will let you hear
the waters sing.
Listen with me . . .

All water moves
in rhythmic tides
from hidden stream
to largest sea.
The mysteries of the lunar tides
Astonish me!

Creation taking place each day,
these water vapors lift and play.
The working plan
we cannot see.
Wait with me!

For my good friends and neighbors who watched
and wondered . . . 1994

❧ THE DRY WALL ❧

Until you build a wall
stone upon stone
and scuff your thumb
and bruise a bone
what you've begun
is still unknown.

A pleasant chat with passers-by
reveals
your talent
does not lie
in building walls.

But, stone upon stone
uneven, unplumbed
these time-stained rocks
seem to say,
"Do not hurry life away."

Imperfect as it seems to be—
the wall, unfinished
has a hold on me.

⇗ WIND BLOWN—FOR C. H. ⇖

She sows the seed
with no regard,
no plan, design—a random yard.
Wind, sun and rain
come on as needed
to stir the dormant earth as seeded.

The flowers bloom and rabbits feed
from fragrant petal
and noxious weed.

Soon frost and snow will blanket all
as winter's reach embraces fall.
Mother Nature saved the day:
the sower puts her trowel away!

❧ THE STORM ❧

Steadily my known world
disappears.
As the snow quickens,
thickens,
the winds shift.
Snow-covered stones,
docile creatures on the lawn.
The path is gone.
The Christmas cake,
crumbed to meet the need
of fly-by visitors
come to feed.
Contained in this
white envelope, I see
a deep contentment
rides this storm
and finds a resting place
in me.

≈ GIFTS ≈

By moonlight
the shadow of the winter birch
drew careful lines
across snow upon snow.

By early morning
the track of deer, rabbit, squirrel
left puzzles to be solved
in the glazed glinting snow.

By late afternoon, twilight perhaps
the barred owl was there.
He came silently, sat motionless
studying the tunnels of the vole,
the mole or the mouse
living inside a hollowed-out log.

All this from the window
of my house—these gifts.

When the owl flew, the
beauty took my breath.
I called—come back!
Perhaps—not yet!

Hold back!
Wait until an unexpected rain
has damped the earth
and winds have, one more time,
chased red and gold and purpling leaves
across the field
against the old rock wall.

Don't bury all of autumn—
not quite yet.
Such letting go
presses against my soul,
a place the harvest moon
has yet to reach.

Stay—not forever—but stay
'til winter's cupboard is filled
with all the garnered grains it needs
to keep us safe
to keep hearts warm
to see us through the days,
the nights
of winter's storm.

⤳ KALEIDOSCOPE ⤳

The summer garden is spent
but not altogether.
The late August heat
brought an outburst
of weather.

Raw winds and rain
tested every last stand
of flower and foliage;
it pounded the land.

As I work through the tumble,
as I mulch I recall
the purples and yellows
of summer and fall.
I know this to be
the beginning—not ending.

I tug at the weeds;
bright packets of seeds
come into view.
Spring, too!

≈ PATTERNS ≈

Anticipation of the bird in flight
    stirs the spirits
    tests the patience:
Wait for light!

Slightly ruffled feathers
    catch the eye,
    a chattered take-off
    chases darkness;
Then the fly!

The rhythm and the power
of the swell; the beauty
but, the awkward grackle
stays aloft, as well!

No pattern quite repeated:
    dip of swallow wings
    webbed feet churning
    the pond's surface,
    rings upon rings.

These aero-dynamics,
a wonder to us all.
No less to me
the earliest pre-dawn call.

ALINA LODGE—1986

The maples drank the orange-red cup.
The oaks put on their richest brown.
The rains blew in and washed the woods
and brought some color down.
The empty nest, the broken branch,
the drift of leaves, the darkening day—
all this called forth November's broom
and swept October
clean
away!

⤝ NOVEMBER ⤞

like the underside
of a handsome garment,
the finest weave,
the rich design,
a wine woolen
with broken threads
and a velvet collar.

November--

Wrap me in your melancholy.
The early darkness
tells me—night is long.

➳ NEW DAY SONNET 1988 ➳

I watched for morning,
when it came
it entered by another name.
The stars and moon, like shepherds led
soft wisps of cloud to
nighttime's bed whose coverlet,
a roseate throw of Eastern light
was slowly letting go the night.
My tangled dreams like questions seeped
out of the folded dark of sleep.
The wonder of creation lay
along the broken edge of day.
Earth's balance wheel brings muted power
to touch my soul this breathless hour.
Alive, awake I shout the praise of God
who gives this gift of days.

≈ THE TREE—1996 ≈

Beauty and complexity
this describes the common tree.
Shelter for the nesting birds,
the Ancients often used the words—
"Tree of knowledge, Tree of life".

The Psalmist wrote:
"All the wood
     rejoiced
and that was good!"

TWO

"AND THEN THERE WAS EVENING"

1967

Familiar

Winter

7 a.m. Haiku

Sleepless in Atlanta

Flyway—1986

Biography

Letter to a Friend—HTR

Pipetunes—1991

Letter to a Dear One—1993

Shadowlight—1985

Pole Star

1967

Washed in winter brightness
I stepped into the day—
my self-bound soul forgot the latch;
my spirit sailed away!

FAMILIAR

Known by my heartbeat
the light from my household
waits my late return.

WINTER

The bamboo, laden with fresh snow
remembering summer,
bends and sways in the raw wind
waiting for the green moss,
the frog's carpet.

SEVEN A.M. HAIKU

The sun breaking
over my neighbor's roof
reminds me
my egg is in the pan.

❧ SLEEPLESS IN ATLANTA 1979 ❧

To my neighbor Margaret's cat—Springlake Place

White Cat, White Cat
of the night
dozing
in the postern light.
The only sound
a cricket's tune.
The distant solitary moon
bathes the image
still as stone.
White Cat, White Cat
you alone
keep the secrets
guiltless, known.
White Cat, White Cat
stay and be
beautiful enough for me.

FLYWAY—1986

Fears came in the night—
the doubts, the dread,
uncertain of the
hiding place of fright.

Then, the wild geese flew;
dawn was only edging up.
The wind was high
and with the call,
remembering, I knew
to open wide the window
and I—let fear fly!

✎ BIOGRAPHY ✎

Tucked in cozily at Wuthering Heights
on the Yorkshire moors
those eerie nights
did the sisters snuggle and read in bed
while Bramwell followed where opium led?

What of tyrant fathers to little girls
chasing them into places of pain?
What of little girls writing verse
finding their own way out again?

Perhaps our world is a better place
but, if it is it isn't so
because the fathers have
changed that much.
Where does each generation go?

LETTER TO A FRIEND—HTR

If you were
      a late summer day—
this day, perfect as it is,
      is not you.
Closing the door
quietly on darkness
you would gentle
across the distant hills
allowing the light and mist
to scatter
      as they please.
The clouds are lambs.
You do not stay
      a thunderstorm,
drenched and washed anew
the western sky
      is purple-red, is purple-blue.

PIPETUNES 1991

To celebrate an original piece of art in the home of R. & K. D.

Let the wind
find a song
to twist and whistle
the tune.

Lilting morning notes
burst and scatter
toward the sun.

Piping away
the edge of day
dusk rides on spirit wings
slipping into the chamber's
inky cell.

One whispered note escapes;
it hovers close
to light the candle:

> we eat
> we rest
> and then
> a sweet amen . . .

Those deaths, that journey
I have taken.
Convinced I was,
fearful and shaken.
I thought I took each death alone
into the darkness, the unknown.
Now, looking back
to that which died
(gnawing and buried deep inside)
my attendant Spirit
was my guide.

My eyes were opened.
I hadn't known.
This trip one never makes alone!

SHADOWLIGHT—1985

The darkness and light
contesting.
Flight brought us here,
flight and fear.

We bend and sway
like shadow boxers
chasing night and day.

A mime appears clothed as
yin and yang.
Regrettably, there is no
place to hang
his magic sword.

The work is ours to do;
cut through to reality;
to name and claim
Our dual selves
and have the wit to
make them fit.

Webster's: a guiding principle

The tree is trimmed with
gifts of every season:

> The gathered daffodils of spring,
> the sudden flash of summer
> on the wing,
> an autumn wind,
> brings color spewing down,
> winter stars flung for an icy crown.

The tree is trimmed
to celebrate all persons
who hold the gift of self
within the soul—
the birth, the life, the death
of each existence,
the gift the gathered celebrants
all hold.

THREE

FOR THE YOUNG AND THE YOUNG IN HEART

The Fairy Godmother:
"I have no time to grow old,
I am too busy for that.
It is very idle to grow old."

from George Macdonald's
Golden Key

Ah-So

Summer Moon

Arc—Angel for NCS

Waking—for KFS

A Letter to Libraries

Adieu

Winter Fashions

Winter Cruise

Touchstone

AH-SO

The poet needs
a tiny cup
to dip the rhymes
and verses up
out of the deep wells
of the soul.
And then for tea
to take a sip
as thoughts unfold.

Forgive my deeds and words today
if they puzzle you.
Tomorrow I will be myself,
the self you thought you knew.
I'll do the usual proper thing
and be the maiden mild
but not today
No! for today
I am April's child.

So, if I skip instead of walk
and wear a lilac in my hair
when I sing and laugh and talk
ignoring every worldly care,
please do not frown
and call my spirit
unbridled and quite wild
for just today—I am sixteen:
today, I'm April's child!

☙ SUMMER MOON ❧

The moon plays a game
as I lay* in my bed:
I have a pillow
for resting my head.
The moon
uses clouds
to cover her face
and stars
mark the path
to moon's pillow
in space.

*lay as in "now I lay me down to sleep"

Like a raindrop
he's the splash!
Body poised to make a dash
as Batman, Robin Hood,
and then, he's daddy's
little boy again!
New worlds created
fresh and bright
he sets a spirit into flight.
Combining color
with the spark
like a rainbow
he's the ARC!

WAKING—KFS

Small warm children
leave their beds
as softly
as the stars disappear.
They whisper
and they peep at
grown-up eyes
to measure sleep.

The silent sun
sends scattered light.
Small children
stretch to push away
the night.

The robin in the birdbath
gives a shake.
She likes to bathe
before small children wake.

When she feels
their eyes
she flies!

⤜ A LETTER TO LIBRARIES ⤛

When I heard that cities
were too poor to keep
libraries open to the public
I couldn't put it out of my mind.

I thought of the nouns
and prepositions and
the little punctuation marks—
with no work to do!
The reference library,
so rich with information,
obscure wonders of the world,
maps, globes and the smell
of books rarely opened.

The quiet of the reading room,
the old man dozing behind a magazine,
students searching for truth
or whispering among the stacks—
maybe falling in love
somewhere between Dante and Donne.

I thought of Sarah
with her nimble mind
and all the knowledge
catalogued for her use.

I thought of myself, a student,
working summers 9 to 5
in a basement of the public library
learning to rebind the broken backs,
to renumber, to repair.
I can still feel the cool of
the quiet cell in which we worked . . .
the smell of the hot glue
comes back to me as I write.

When I heard that cities
were too poor to keep
libraries open to the public
I thought of Sarah
and all other Sarahs
and of myself.

⫷ ADIEU ⫸

Living in the "fix-it" age
at seventy she reached the stage
CONSIDER: Win, Place or Show.
The guarantee was "No".
"Wrinkle-Out too late for me?
In twenty years I'm bound to be
ashes to ashes
and wrinkle free!

☙ WINTER FASHIONS ❧

Layering is the dress code here.
Always begin next to the skin with
something that breathes, something thin
T-shirts, turtlenecks
blue jeans and sweater,
topped off with a windbreaker,
couldn't be better.
But,
somewhere buried,
warm and fat
is where the
original body's at!

❧ WINTER CRUISE ❧

The shamelessness of her flirtation
Has put them all in fits.
She's taken rules from every book
And broken them to bits!

Her laughter in the public rooms
Is getting darker stares
From the other ladies present
Than stow-aways, in pairs.

She has charmed the solemn purser
To the uttermost degree.
He simply oozed with helpfulness
When she lost her stateroom key.

Her figure is no miracle
And her wardrobe not the best.
With WHAT engaging magic
Is this female menace blessed?

The reason that it's galling
And I'm raising such a fuss—
Back home, in Pennsylvania
She's the girl next door to us!

TOUCHSTONE

Confessing
that I like the tasks
ordinary living asks
along the way,
        I mark my day.
The early morning
empty of sound
until sun, wind and cloud
surround
each motion and each step
I take . . .
What work to read,
tune to sing?
Each simple effort
seems to bring
a truth to which
I must agree:
        I'm cared for:
        a do-nothing-me!

✳✳✳✳✳✳✳✳✳✳✳